THE ENERGY DYNAMIC MODEL

THE ANSWER

PART 1

JENNIFER FOSTER MA BSC

BookVenture Publishing LLC
1000 Country Lane Ste 300
Ishpeming MI 49849
www.bookventure.com
Hotline: 1(877) 276-9751
Fax: 1(877) 864-1686

Ordering Information:
Quantity sales. Special discounts are available on quantity purchases by corporations, associations, and others. For details, contact the publisher at the address above.

Printed in the United States of America.

Library of Congress Control Number		2017947582
ISBN-13:	Softcover	978-1-64069-328-9
	Pdf	978-1-64069-329-6
	ePub	978-1-64069-330-2
	Kindle	978-1-64069-331-9

Rev. date: 07/12/2017

Dedicated to my mother.

Note to Reader

This is the first book in the Energy Dynamic model series. The series is all about a new way to understand how people have had to adapt to deal with modern society. Although this model has only recently been developed, what it explains is not really new. The ability to be a powerful and creative human being is inherent in us all and has been ever since we were cavemen. What the 'Energy Dynamic' model does is to remind and show you how to access this knowledge which has become buried and forgotten today.

The idea is based on research gathered up by the author who tied together three different strands of data that took twenty-five years to collate. About 20% of the information was found by studying Economics and Philosophy up to a Master's degree level, approximately 20% of the information was found by direct personal experience but by far the most data was collected by working directly with over two and a half thousand people including people with learning difficulties, mental health problems, social workers, nurses, therapists, spiritual practitioners, doctors, business people, long term unemployed, millionaires, families and youngsters. The life stories of these people were carefully considered and then noted down. Special attention was given to how they described 'who they were', how they experienced life and how their mind worked.

By putting together patterns and similarities that cropped up from this data, the 'Energy Dynamic' model was finally completed in 2010. This first book 'The Answer' was written as a dialogue between two characters discussing the development of the idea.

The second book, called 'The I in the Storm' is very different in nature to the first one. Finished in 2015, the aim is to give people a simple structure which can be used to understand how people operate in this modern world, in an *intuitive way. There is no need for any knowledge about psychology or science to understand this idea. All you need is your imagination and an open mind. A whole new language and way of seeing things will be introduced to you through this book and new words created to help you reconstruct how you think about and see yourself and other people.*

In 2017, an online Academy was set up by Jennifer so that people could deepen their knowledge of the Energy Dynamic model and have access to one to one support via email and training in applying the methodology to their own unique self and situation. Based entirely on these two books, the online 'Intuitive Way To Understand People' program is highly recommended for people who enjoy this new concept and who want to bring the ideas contained in these pages, alive.

All topics are covered in this program including managing stress, teaching children and young people how to be strong, understanding mental health conditions and leadership.

To enrol in the online Academy, just visit the Energy Dynamic website. This can be found at www.energydynamic.co.uk.

The Answer

A One Act Play

Act 1

'Energy'

'Without energy a human being can not carry on living. They slowly die. The difference between a dead person and an alive one is not what caused the death itself, but the fact that the person did not have enough energy to heal.....'

'Prospero'.....Act 1 Scene 1

Act 1

Scene 1

Two men are sitting in a pub garden with drinks. It is a drizzly day and they are sheltering in a stone enclave built in the wall surrounding the garden. There is ivy growing around the enclave and small purple flowers nesting in the crumbling stone wall. Both men are facing the same way, looking out over the lawn. They are huddled up, curled around their drinks. The rain makes it hard to see anything. A water fountain and an ornamental fish pond lurk in the middle distance. The only sounds that can be heard are the rain drops tapping the ivy leaves and the quiet gurgle of the water fountain. The men, however, do not seem to notice the rain or the damp. They are deep in conversation. The older one, Prospero, is speaking quite loudly and passionately to the other younger man, Boy.

Prospero: *(In an agitated manner, pointing his finger to make his point).* So, you see, Boy, people are wanting to know the Answer. *(Pause. Boy looks puzzled).* The Answer to what? You may well ask, my dear Boy! The Answer to what indeed... *(Scowls).* The Answer to Everything, of course. What exactly do the people need to know the Answer to Everything for? Think, Boy, think. Look around and see! *(Prospero leans back and looks expectantly at Boy).*

Boy: *(Hesitantly).* I have no idea, Sir...

Prospero: *(Speaking more softly).* They want to know the Answer to Everything, because they have forgotten what they are here for. They have no memory! No idea of what is going on! *(Whispering).* They need the Answer to Everything so that they can be motivated enough to simply get out of bed in the morning. *(Looks at Boy and pauses).* Why? Because they need this Answer to give their lives a sense of purpose and meaning! *(Takes a gulp from his drink).* They are fools. All of them!

Boy: *(Cautiously).* Prospero, do you mean the people have forgotten something important? So, they need the Answer to Everything to make up for this? And this Answer gives them what they are looking for? *(Leans back).* Sounds logical. Not foolish! *(Pause).* Is this what you mean?

Prospero: *(Waving his arms around to make his point).* Yes, Boy, it is logical because it gives them a direction. But it is also foolish, because they are not looking at what they are being directed towards. *(Patiently).* And Boy *(moving closer to Boy),* this so called direction actually takes people away from what they have forgotten about in the first place! This so called direction takes them into a space which is diametrically opposite to where they need to be. They do not realise this! *(He sighs and looks over the garden).* *(Looks at Boy. Begins to speak slowly).* Let me start at the beginning. *(Sighs again).*

Boy: *(Earnestly).* I am listening!

Prospero: Then listen hard and hear me well. Pay attention. *(Leans back in his chair).*

About forty years ago, most people who lived in this part of the planet suddenly started to discover that their lives, their lives as defined by themselves, had become, almost overnight, without any purpose or meaning. Imagine that, Boy! Suddenly, out of nowhere, discovering this. *(He leans towards Boy).* People started to experience a feeling of absolute Nothingness in their day to day life. They started to realise that they were actually living in a permanent state of feeling Nothingness.......

Boy: Feeling Nothingness?

Prospero: A desperate place to be in for any animal or soul. The leaders of the countries in this part of the world saw what was happening to the people. *(Dramatically).* The leaders decided that this terrible problem had to be solved. Immediately! Never mind the cause! The Nothingness must go! *(Starts to speak like a robot).* 'It is impossible for a human being to exist with this Nothingness feel; if this Nothingness feel is inside a man, he may well be overcome by it. He will be in danger of becoming inactive.' *(Boy looks at Prospero* *as if he must be joking).* Boy, you must pay attention to this! *(Prospero starts to speak in the robot voice again).* 'This Nothingness plague, if not taken seriously, could mean the destruction of human kind. This Nothingness must be dealt with… A solution to the feeling of Nothingness must be found!' *(Sits back again, laughing and banging the glass on the table. He starts to mimic a judge in court, using the same robot voice. He speaks louder and louder).* 'We must get rid of this Nothingness feeling. We must find a remedy for this. A Somethingelseness must be created! A Somethingelseness must be found to halt the spread of this dangerous Nothingness!'

Boy: *(Who has been listening to all this intently).* Somethingelseness?

Prospero: *(He starts to pace around the small enclave and bends towards Boy as he starts to whisper the next sentence).* Somethingelseness was thought up by the leaders. They realised that this plague of Nothingness could cause huge disruption to the social and economic system. *(Pause).*

Boy, this was a big challenge for them! If no action was taken to tackle the phenomenon, huge numbers of the population would be prone to 'death by apathy'. *(Looking pensive).* Significant problems for society, and disruption to the status quo. *(Robot voice again).* 'This must not be allowed to happen!' *(He suddenly looks very serious).* The leaders needed their people active and busy, Boy. What could they do? How could they achieve this? *(Prospero pauses to take a drink. He wipes his mouth with his hand. He offers Boy a packet of nuts and sits down at the table again.)* Have a nut, Boy. *(Pause. They eat their nuts nosily. Prospero speaks softly).* The leaders had to come up with a solution. And they did, Boy. A very clever one indeed. But I must warn you, now. *(He looks around and talks with an exaggerated whisper).* An Answer was found. Yes, indeed. But the Answer was not born alone, Boy. The Answer came with a secret. A very important secret. The Secret, in fact…… *(He winks at Boy and looks around quickly).*

Boy: *(Surprises).* A secret? The Secret! What secret, Sir?

Prospero: The Secret, Boy. The Secret of the Answer. *(Pause. Laughs.)* The Secret of the Answer, Boy, is that the Answer was made up. Made up. Made up by the…..

Boy*: (Interrupts, shocked).* The Answer! Made up? Are you serious Prospero?

Prospero*:* Absolutely Boy. Think about it. *(Prospero sits back and seems to relax).* The leaders didn't know what was causing this Nothingness feeling. Or maybe they didn't care. (*Whispering*). It didn't really matter. The important point for them was to keep the population going. They had to stop the people feeling Nothingness somehow. *(Pause).* So, they decided to create an answer to this problem themselves. Boy, they just decided to make something up that would mean the people would become active and productive again. The leaders just wanted the people to be productive, my Boy, remember that. Nothing more, nothing less. People are human energy stores. Energy stores produce. Production must continue. End of mystery.

Boy: Crikey!

Prospero: Yes, indeed. *(He finishes off the peanuts. Relaxes).* The answer the leaders came up with was the idea of Somethingelseness. *(Prospero pauses for effect and stands up to pronounce this in his robot voice).* 'My People. Great news. We have found a solution to the Apathy plague. A new Somethingelseness has been discovered! This Somethingelseness will give us reasons, purposes, to live for! *(Pause).* It is called the 'Answer to Everything'. *(Prospero raises his glass).* Everybody stand. Three cheers for Somethingelseness! Three cheers for our Answer! Three cheers for our new motivational goal! We will all be able to get up out of bed and run about in the morning again. We have found the solution! All is well. Nothingness is dead; long live the Answer! Hip hip hooray!' *(Prospero sits down again, and starts speaking in his normal voice. Long pause).* And the people were very grateful to the leaders, Boy. They began to enjoy this Somethingelseness experience. Instead of suffering Nothingness, they found Somethingelseness. Slowly the situation changed. People started to find some energy. They began to think they were better. They started to do things again. They stopped staring into space wondering what on earth was happening to them and what the Nothingness meant. They believed that they felt all right. And so, they did! Have you got that Boy? Yes? The people thought it worked. This is very important. The people completely believed in the Answer because it made them think that they were fine again. And they were fine, because they believed that this was so. *(Pause. Slowly).* But now, however, there was also a Secret. The Secret was the fact that the Answer was all made up by the….(*Looks around as the rain suddenly gets heavier).* Remember this, Boy. It is important for later on. Good. More nuts? *(He takes another packet out of his pocket and offers them to Boy, who takes some. It starts to rain more heavily).*

Boy*:* Yes, thank you, Sir.

Prospero*: (Pulling his coat around him a bit more).* Now then, Boy, the next question is..

Why did this work? Why on earth would it? Why would creating something extra and, don't forget, actually from pure fantasy; get rid of something that was already there and absolutely real? *(Pause. Looks at Boy).*

Boy*:* I have no idea Prospero….

Prospero*: (Smirking).* Well, Boy, you see, actually, it didn't.

Boy*:* But…..

Prospero*: (Impatient).* The Secret of the Answer! The Answer is made up. It is not the solution for Nothingness. The people just believed it was. It does not take away the Nothingness feeling. *(Excitedly).* But it does appear to. It is a trick, it is a distraction. The Nothingness appears to disappear. But it is still there, it is just not noticed! The Answer creates Somethingelseness, Boy. Pure and simple! *(Gulps some drink).* It is a piece of human magic, of deception. *(Bends towards Boy again).* And the trick worked. It worked because the nature of the Somethingelseness distracts from the

Nothingness feeling. It was perfect. Very, very clever Boy. *(Pause).* I'll show you. *(He uses a beer mat and beer glass to illustrate this).* This is Nothingness….the beer mat…. and this is Somethingelseness….the beer glass. The Somethingelseness gets rid of the empty Nothingness feeling by hiding it. *(He puts the beer glass over the beer mat).* You can't see the Nothingness anymore, can you? And the beer glass part of this trick is, well, genius. So. Watch now. Not only does the beer glass hide the beer mat, the Nothingness, but it also makes the people completely forget that the beer mat was ever even there! *(Pauses for effect).* How does it do this? Well, by filling the beer glass up with 'something else'. Something else which appears to give the people what they think they need. The people, once drinking from the beer glass, start to forget about what they are missing, the Nothingness feeling. They start to fill themselves up with the new alternative. *(Drinks some beer. Pause. Standing up again and pronouncing to the imaginary crowd in his robot voice again).* 'People, look at the beer glass. And drink from what lies within it... *(In a sinister fashion).* Forget about the beer mat! The beer mat Nothingness creates apathy. Who wants that? Well, no one of course. *(Upbeat again).* Come and find the Answer. Do Somethingelseness instead! Drown out the Nothingness... Find Somethingelseness instead! Bottoms up! *(Prospero downs his pint).*

Boy*:* Goodness me, Prospero!

Prospero*: (Smiles to his imaginary audience and sits down).* How the drink in the beer glass takes all the attention away from the beer mat, Boy, is even more interesting.... *(Abruptly stops. He stares menacingly at Boy).* But before I tell you more, I must buy us another one. Same again, I assume?

Prospero turns on his heels and marches off through the garden. The rain has nearly stopped now and his footprints make damp markings in the grass. He disappears from view as he turns left. A few minutes later he returns with two more drinks in his hand. Boy has spent the time looking at some notes he has found in his pocket. As Prospero approaches, he puts these hastily back into his pocket.

Prospero: So. *(Settling down in his seat and arranging his long overcoat around him).* Have you any ideas, Boy, about how this might have worked? How the Nothingness feeling could be hidden by and apparently obliterated by the Somethingelseness effect?

Boy: No, Sir. None at all. Seems all quite intriguing though I must say.

Prospero: *(Hands Boy his drink and starts to sip his own).* Good. Well, in order to explain more, I will have to take you back even further into the human being's social and evolutionary history. Years before the Answer was found, years before people had the Nothingness feel…

Boy: Great!

Prospero: So, imagine this. *(Pause).* Imagine that years and years ago, just after the human beings were created, they felt pretty good most of the time carrying on with their day to day activities. Keep that thought Boy, but update into our conversation. Think carefully Boy. *(Pause).* Let us play a game. What would you say is the best way to get rid of a 'feel' of Nothingness? Think upside down Boy. Start with the best way to get rid of a 'feeling' in general. *(Prospero smiles and starts to play with a fallen ivy leaf).* Let's use this. Assume plants can 'feel'. What would be the quickest and most certain way to stop this ivy plant here on the wall from feeling sad because it is missing this ivy leaf that has fallen onto the table, Boy? Use your brain. *(Prospero grins and crumbles the leaf in his hand and lets it drop)....*

Boy: *(Frowns).* Tell me, Sir, I'm not sure at all...

Prospero: *(Looking at the crumbled leaf).* By killing the plant. *(Pause. He sips some of his drink and stares at Boy).*

Boy: Oh no. *(Decidedly).* No. That wouldn't work Prospero. If you killed the plant, then, yes, the plant would not feel sad. That part is true. But the plant would be dead! That would be self defeating and pointless. If there was no plant then, fair enough, there would be no 'feel', but there would also be no leaves, no actual ivy plant or even any 'ivy' type of existence. *(Pause).* That would not happen. That does not make good biological sense, Prospero. No.

Prospero*: (Nodding).* Very good, Boy. It would indeed be destructive and would lead to the extinction of ivy, meaning the extinction of the very thing that we are trying to keep going. Therefore this would not happen. Nature would not allow it. Very good. *(Pause).* But it is to do with this. Try again….

Boy*:* I'm not sure…

Prospero*:* Be more precise. We would need to destroy the part of the plant that would know that there was something missing. The very part of the plant that would feel the sad feeling…..

Boy*: (Impatiently).* But that's not possible, Sir. By destroying the part of the plant that could 'feel', surely you would be destroying the very essence of the plant? You would be destroying the whole purpose of the plant, of the being.

Prospero: No, no, Boy. That is an assumption. You are assuming that the part that can 'feel' is the essence of the plant. It is not. However, to go back a step. If it was possible to destroy the part of the plant that could feel, without obliterating the plant... Would that work? Boy, listen. Imagine.

Boy: (*Puzzled again*). I am struggling...

Prospero: (*Speaking slowly and with intensity*). Say there is more to the plant than just its 'feel'. Say you could get rid of the 'feel' of the plant but that you were able to, at the same time, still keep the actual plant alive. Say it was possible to keep the plant alive but take away all 'feeling' of anything, whatever that 'feeling' was. Consider this, Boy....

Boy: I'm doing my best Prospero. Let me work this out. (*Leans back, concentrates very hard*). Is this what you are saying? The 'feel' part of a living being is not the essence of the very self of a living being. It is a part of it, an important part, but not the defining essence. Therefore, it could be theoretically possible to keep an ivy plant in existence, without the 'feel', because the essence of the plant would still be contained within the actual plant. If this is true, then theoretically you could have ivy plants existing that do not 'feel'. Ivy plants that actually would not be able to 'feel' anything at all. If we apply this to our original puzzle, then this would mean that the ivy plant would indeed not be able to feel sadness, because they would not have a 'feeling' to experience the sadness with......

Prospero: *(Looking impressed)*. Excellent, Boy, that is precisely what I am saying. That it is theoretically possible to have a living being in existence, with 'itself' intact (whatever that may be), even though it can not 'feel'. Yes. Very good.

Boy: Right, I'm with you now....

Prospero: *(Speaking carefully and with precision)*. But, Boy, the reason that this is important and relevant, is that although the living being can theoretically exist with no 'feel', it can not sustain itself for very long in this 'non feeling' state….

Boy*: (Disappointed).* Oh no, well, the problem can't be solved then! To just exist in a space of time is not enough; we need the ivy plant, or the 'being', to be sustainable, to be able to live. *(Interestedly).* But tell me, why does no 'feeling' mean a living being can not sustain itself?

Prospero*:* Because of this natural law, Boy. Let me write it down and then I will explain.

Prospero digs into his coat pocket and finds a crumbled piece of paper and a pen. He writes the following down on the paper, which he keeps from becoming damp by using a beer mat to lean on. The sun has started to peer out from the grey clouds and the whole of the beer garden becomes dappled with spotted sunlight.

LAW 1

ORGANISMS NEED ENERGY TO LIVE.
THEY NEED THIS MORE THAN
THEY NEED FOOD AND WATER TO
FEED FROM, OR OXYGEN TO
BREATH WITH, OR SHELTER TO
REST IN.

Boy: *(Taking the piece of paper from Prospero when he is offered it and reads it, squinting in the light).* Energy? What does energy have to do with this?

Prospero: *(Eating peanuts and drinking his beer again).* Absolutely everything! It is the most fundamental need of all life.

Boy: *(Putting down the paper).* It may well be. But we were talking about having no 'feel'. Are they linked?

Prospero: *(Laughing).* Yes, of course. They are indeed. They are inseparable. *(Pretends to be a teacher by pointing to Boy and behaving as if he has a class of pupils).* Now, listen everyone and pay attention. Human beings need energy to become alive and to sustain themselves. This energy is gathered up by them as they go about their day, feeling good about themselves. This energy is stored in their Power Energy Store. However. *(Pause).* If the 'feel' part of the person is not working properly, the human beings can not gather up energy in this way.

Boy*: (Laughing and drinking)* Goodness me, Sir.

Prospero*: (Becoming himself again).* Let's look at these human beings in more detail. Let us start by dividing them up into the parts that make them up. *(Starts to point to the plants and to draw pictures in the air with his hands as he speaks).* Assume that the human being operates in the same way as the ivy plant. What a human being 'feels' is not the same at all as their very essence. Let us call this essence of the human being 'who they are'. So, a human being's 'feel' is to do with their energy function; it is completely separate to 'who they are' which is to do with how they are created as themselves, how they are a unique individual. *(Pauses. Looks intently at Boy).* Are you with me?

Boy*: Yes, I think so….*

Prospero*: (Continues in earnest. Stands up again and starts to pace).* Now consider this. Human beings can not live without energy, Boy. They need energy more than they need food. It is as essential to them as water. Without energy a human being can not carry on living. They slowly die. The difference between a dead person and an alive one is not what caused the death itself, but that the deceased person did not have enough energy to heal. Can you understand this?

Boy*: (Seriously).* Yes, Prospero. But if that is the case, when a person has no 'feel'….

Prospero*:* Good. Be quiet. *(Sits down and writes the following on another piece of paper found in his pocket).* The second law is as follows:

LAW 2

HUMAN BEINGS HAVE THREE WAYS OF GATHERING UP ENERGY – THE 'SPIRITUAL' ENERGY WAY, THE 'BEING YOU' ENERGY WAY AND THE 'MIND' ENERGY WAY. THE 'MIND' ENERGY WAY IS THE WEAKEST METHOD AND HAS BEEN DEVELOPED IN RECENT TIMES (FROM THE 1930S ONWARDS).

Boy: *(Reading the 'law' out loud as he reads it after Prospero hands it to him).* Hmmm. There are three ways of finding energy. Well, that's a relief then. For a moment I thought that if human beings could not 'feel', then that was the end of that. They wouldn't be able to gather up any energy!

Prospero: *(Ironically).* Yes indeed, Boy. Thank goodness, eh?

Boy: So, *(reading from the paper again),* which one of these three ways of gathering energy relates to the 'feel' part?

Prospero: *(Leaning back, relaxing slightly and seeming to enjoy the sunlight as he puts up his hands to partly shade his eyes).* The 'Being You' energy is the feeling energy. It is how you have experienced being you, in the situations that you have been in. How a person 'feels' Boy, is all to do with the state of their Power Energy Store. If this is full of 'good feelings' or peace, the person will experience this as a general state of contentedness. If this is full of 'sad feelings' or grief, the person will experience this as heaviness, hollowness and lethargy. *(Puts his hand down rather suddenly).* Also, please note, Boy. This grief is strong enough to overwhelm the other types of energy. A person can not live if their Power Energy Store is filled with grief, as they will eventually be overwhelmed by their sad feelings and will not be able to carry on.

Boy: *(Listening carefully).* Goodness me. What causes these contented or grief feeling states in your Power Energy Store?

Prospero: Good question. Have you got any spare paper? *(Boy shakes his head).* Here you go then... *(He pulls out a scruffy* *notepad from his big overcoat pocket and slaps it on the table in front of Boy. He pulls out a pen too).* Write this down. *(He seems to relax more, slightly shutting his eyes against the weak sunlight and starts to speak slowly).* More facts about energy. Energy is always the same in its purest form; it is not 'good' or 'bad'. When it is existing in an isolated state in the universe somewhere, energy just 'is'. However, as soon as it interacts with human beings, it changes and can be experienced in different ways. The feeling energy becomes either good which leads to peace, or sad which leads to grief….

Boy*:* Why? *(Scribbling fast).*

Prospero*:* Wait boy. Wait now. *(Opens his eyes and becomes focused on Boy again).* Remember the 'who you are' part of a human being? Well, this is where that all fits in. If, when you are being 'who you are' in day to day life, your Power Needs register an overall 'yes', you will have a good feeling, or in other words a 'plus' energy experience. If, however, you are 'who you are' in day to day life and your Power Needs register an overall 'no', you will have a sad feeling, or in other words a 'minus' energy experience.........

Boy: *(Struggling to write this all down).* Right, so you are saying that the feeling energy is either a 'plus' or a 'minus' depending on what happens to your Power Needs when you are being 'who you are' in day to day life. *(Looks at Prospero).* But what are Power Needs exactly?

Prospero: *(Impatiently).* I will talk more about them later on, Boy. For now I just want you to understand the general principle here...

Boy: *(Looking back at notes).* Yes, I think I do. The energy that the human beings gather up from their feelings is accessed from the energy that exists in the universe somewhere else, separately, in a pure form. Once this energy is found by a human being, it is experienced as a 'plus' feel, if, when you gather up this energy by being 'who you are' in day to day life, your Power Needs are an overall 'yes'. Or, gathering up energy in this way can be experienced as a 'minus' feel, if, when you are 'who you are' in your day to day life, your Power Needs are an overall 'no'........

Prospero*: Indeed.*

Boy*: …..And if the human being has too many minus 'feels', then they will be slowly overwhelmed by this feeling which would eventually mean that they die. They will not be able to heal themselves. This feeling is described as overwhelming grief…. (Looks up triumphantly at Prospero).*

Prospero*: (Prospero pauses while he scratches with a pebble on the table).* Excellent. Very good. Right. So, where are we?

Boy*: (Becoming more confident now).* Let me recap once more Prospero. Now then. Human beings need to survive. They are living beings. They need energy to be alive and sustain themselves. This can be accessed from the universe in three different ways. The method which accesses energy in the strongest way is from the 'Being You' way, or in other words, how you 'feel'. Your feelings are stored in your Power Energy Store. This is experienced by the human beings as either a 'plus' feeling or a 'minus' feeling. Good feelings result in a feeling of peace, sad feelings result in a feeling of grief. If, unfortunately, because of 'who they are' in their day to day life, too many minus feelings are gathered up, the human being will experience overwhelming grief in their Power Energy Store. So, they will need to stop feeling this grief, because if they do not, they will be in danger of being drowned from within by these sad feelings! *(Pause).* However, Prospero, at the same time, the human beings need energy everyday to live! And they can not sustain themselves, day to day, if they are only gathering up sad feeling energy. *(Puts the notepad down).* How's that then?

Prospero*:* Very good, Boy. Tell me again why gathering up minus feeling energy is dangerous, and what the human beings must do if this continues for a while.......

Boy*: (Talking to himself and referring to his notes).* Minus feeling energy is dangerous for two reasons. Firstly, because the sad energy within the person could overwhelm them with grief at any time, and secondly, because a person will become very weak if they can only gather up sad feeling energy. *(Thinking).* There are other sources of energy too. But, in order to keep alive they have to get rid of this potentially overwhelming grief filled Power Energy Store pretty quickly. *(Looks again at his notepad).* Hmmmm….Tricky. Hold on though….I've got it! There is only one thing they can do. The ivy plant….They have to get rid of what they 'feel'! They will have to make themselves safe from this potentially overwhelming feeling of grief. So, they will have to stop 'feeling'…?

Prospero: *(Looks impressed).* Excellent, my dear Boy. Yes indeed. They are in danger of being overwhelmed, or in other words, in danger of being drowned from within by the grief filled Power Energy Store. So, they have to turn the water mains off, so to speak. Great. You are doing well with your understanding, Boy.

Boy: *(Proudly).* Thank you, Sir.

Prospero: *(Sitting up straight, shading his eyes from the weak sunshine and looking* *straight at Boy).* Let me elaborate. Let me tell you more. Back into the past again. Until about 80 years ago, Boy, human beings were wandering around with their feelings still intact. Their Power Energy Stores and their day to day generated feelings were all in a plus feeling state. The people felt strong, peaceful and content, just by being alive…. But suddenly, and without people really noticing, many of them started to accumulate minus feeling energy somehow. People's Power Energy Stores started to fill up with sad feelings. They started to become weaker. They started to feel grief. They didn't know what to do! They didn't understand it. *(Long pause).* But Boy, luckily, they didn't have to worry for long. Mother Nature took over. Mother Nature was not having this.

Boy: *(Listening. Drinking his beer).* Really.

Prospero: *(Drinking too).* Oh yes, Boy. Human beings had been around for thousands of years and they hadn't kept going for this long without Mother Nature developing some safety mechanisms. *(Pause).* Mother Nature had an age old way of dealing with the grief problem. Developed over time, this tried and tested survival mechanism kicked in, and what happened next accidentally took the human species into a new developmental stage.

Boy: *(Listening excitedly).* Goodness me!

Prospero: Oh yes. *(Sighs and shakes his head).* Evolution is a funny thing. One of the oldest safety mechanisms, applied in a totally new context, in a totally new era. Very dangerous.

Boy: *(Eating peanuts too).* So, what happened next?

Prospero: *(Leaning back).* The safety mechanism. Right then. *(Sits up again at the table).* The brain, to ensure that human beings could carry on surviving when the Power Energy Store became too full of grief, had developed an emergency action in order to deal with this. Cutting off the person from these feelings would prevent illness and death from overwhelming grief…

Boy: *(Smiling and pleased).* Ha ha! I see! I was right! The ivy plant...'

Prospero: Yes, you were right. *(Staring seriously at Boy).* But please note, as far as the brain was concerned, this was just an emergency, temporary action. And as you now know, human beings need energy to live from, so to cut off the Power Energy Store, the best form of energy, is very dangerous in the long term. *(Pause).* The human being would not really be able to function properly whilst they had no feelings. They would be immobilised. *(Pause. Thoughtfully).* A bit like turning the engine off in a car that was just about to blow up. It will just stop...

Boy: Right. *(Finds the notebook and pen ready and starts scribbling again).* So, the person would still exist, but that would be about it. *(Pauses. Looks at Prospero).* To use the car metaphor again, Sir, the action of turning off the car would save it from blowing up, but the problem causing the situation would have to be sorted out quickly in order for the car to get moving again...

Prospero: *(Nodding his head).* Indeed. Now then, Boy, what do you think being cut off from the feelings could be described as?.

Boy: Let me think. *(Smirking).* I know. I've got it. Could it be Nothingness?

Prospero: *(Clapping).* Brilliant, Boy. Yes. Human beings cut themselves off from their feelings to prevent themselves from being overwhelmed from within by a grief filled Power Energy Store. *(Pause).* However, even though the human being would still continue to exist as a person, (because the essence of the human being 'who they are', is still within that person), they would not be able to function very well. The person would still be present, but with no feelings at all, and with no way of gathering up any feeling energy either. *(Seriously).* Now then, Boy, people who find themselves in this state are starved of feeling energy and can not experience life properly as a feeling human being at all.........

Boy: *(Excitedly).* Yes. My goodness. They will be desperate. They will have to find some sort of alternative energy from somewhere. Or they will die! They will need to find something to keep them going.

Prospero: *(Seriously and frowning)*. Exactly, Boy. The immediate problem of internal drowning from within would be temporarily stalled, but the next challenge is....?

Boy: How to access some alternative energy? How to find some more energy!

Prospero: Yes. Because if you are cut off from your feelings, you can not feel, even if there are good feelings around. *(Pause)*. This next point is very important, Boy. Write this down. *(In teacher role again)*. You can not gather up any feeling energy, even if this energy happens to be a 'plus', if you are in a state of cut off-ness. Being cut off is exactly like turning off the water mains in a house. If dirty water has found its way into the water system and reaches the storage tank you must stop drinking the water and cut off the supply immediately. But once you have turned the mains off, you can not access water from anywhere. So, if and when feelings in the day to day become a 'plus' experience for the person, it is still impossible to gather up this type of energy because the human being remains in a cut off state. No feelings mean no energy for the Power Energy Store. 'Plus' or 'minus'. This is an absolute fact.

Boy*: (Stops scribbling).* What a shame, Prospero. All that potential feeling energy wasted.

Prospero*:* I know, Boy. It is extraordinarily ineffective. However. Human beings create their own terrible mess....*(Pause).* Now then. Are you still paying attention?

Boy*:* Oh yes, I'm all ears Prospero....

Prospero*:* Listen well. *(Change of tone).* I am going to stretch my legs for a bit, Boy, so you listen as I pace. It seems to be turning into a quite beautiful evening now....

Prospero gets up, strokes down his overcoat and walks around the enclave whilst talking, and peers at the flowers in the wall as he speaks. The weak sun is setting and there is indeed a beautiful sunset starting to creep into the overcast sky. A few birds sing as they peck the damp earth, and Prospero watches them hop around, beneath the ornamental waterfall.

In the years gone by, Boy, during the Stone Age period, the brain never used to cut off the Power Energy Store permanently. It was much too dangerous. Not only did the human beings pick up huge amounts of essential energy by gathering up good feelings about 'who they were', but, Boy, if human beings couldn't feel, they couldn't understand basic day to day life either. Once cut off from this feeling energy collection, all the knowledge gained from gathering up energy in this way would be lost as well. Confusion and chaos! *(Pause).* If the Power Energy Store did fall too low and the brain found it necessary to cut off the feelings of the person, this state would probably remain for some time whilst the Power Energy Store levels became safe again. *(Pause).* The brain had a difficult task of balancing up the pros and cons of reconnection, but Boy, these human prehistoric brains knew what they were doing and what was important. And that was to connect up again as soon as possible. *(Earnestly).* These damned human beings needed to have their feelings and knowledge back again!

Boy*: (Head buried in his notes).* Sounds very tricky. And the brain would have to get it right. The longer the human being had no access to the Power Energy Store, the more time they would be out of action. But if the brain connected up too quickly to the energy store, then hey, overwhelming grief meltdown time…

Prospero*:* Exactly Boy. Very difficult to judge. *(Turns to look at Boy. Starts to pace in a different direction).* However, there was a way. The brain managed to do this by allowing brief moments of partial reconnection time, every now and then. A bit like the car we mentioned earlier. Like turning on the ignition after the engine had cooled down to see if it's able to work properly again without overheating. This is exactly how it worked with the human beings. Once the brain decided that the Power Energy Store had settled down; well, enough to avoid an overheating car situation so to speak, the brain would test the situation. *(Pause).* As soon as the person's feelings became a 'plus' in the present, permanent partial reconnection could take place. The 'plus' feelings in the present would start to be gathered up again. A period of recovery would begin, with the person slowly regaining good feelings in the Power Energy Store by going about their normal business. Slowly, but surely, the person would regain a peaceful Power Energy Store. *(Pause).* This would lead to the reconnection becoming more whole, so allowing the person to gather up more energy. So slowly, very slowly, the person would return to their contented state, eventually being peaceful and whole again. *(Pause).* Have you got all this, Boy?

Boy: Yes. *(Stops writing and pauses whilst he reads some back).* It all sounds pretty sensible.

Prospero: *(Standing still and looking around).* Good. Well, shall we leave now? Our drinks are finished and the sun is setting. We can talk once we arrive home.

Boy: Sure, Prospero. Let me just collect my things. (*He starts to gather up the notebook and pen*). But I do have a question, Prospero. I am puzzled by something. How do these strange human beings find any energy when they are disconnected from their feelings? Because if they can't access this energy supply, then surely they would just become immobile. Like the overheated car. They would be just left on the roadside.

Prospero: Yes. (*Talks to Boy as they prepare to leave*). They would indeed be left on the roadside. Extremely dangerous, Boy, for the individual as well as for the society they lived in. A broken down human being is vulnerable to random outside events. Such as being eaten by a passing animal! (*Pause*). And broken down people also demand extra attention and take away resources from others in their tribe. Detrimental for all sorts of reasons. A broken down human being can not hunt, feed children or tend animals.

Boy: No, of course not. (*They both start to leave the table. A bar lady comes out into the garden to turn on the lamp and the patio* *heater. The beer garden lights up).* What happens? Do they just stay still and stuck for days? Do the rest of their tribe put them somewhere special?

Prospero*: (Laughs).* No, not really. You are forgetting something about energy and the human being.

Boy*:* Oh, let me remember. *(Pause).* Hmmmm. Accessing energy. Oh yes, of course. Law number 2. There are three ways of accessing energy.

Prospero*:* Excellent my dear, Boy. Good. Yes. *(Turns around to speak to Boy directly).* Talking of which, shall we eat here? You are so full of questions and this beer garden looks just right now for a leisurely meal with some rather nice red wine……

Boy*:* Oh yes, that would be great. Where shall we sit? *(They both sit on the seats around a table set up for a meal for two prepared by the bar lady).* Thank you. So where was I? Oh yes. So, I assume the broken down human beings would sustain themselves by using another method of gathering up energy?

Prospero: Yes, indeed. *(Looks at the menu and puts it down again)*. During difficult times, if the grief energy became too overwhelming, the Stone Age man was still able to keep going, Boy. *(Pause. Looks at the menu again)*. Even though they may well be disconnected from their feelings, they would still manage ….

Boy: *(Looking at the menu too)*. Sounds awful, Prospero.

Prospero: *(Studying the menu)*. Every day life for these poor human beings, Boy….

Boy: Thankfully, I can only imagine. *(Hands menu back to Prospero)*. How on earth did they manage? What type of energy did they gather up instead?

Prospero: Orders first! Same as before, Boy? *(Looks for the bar lady who catches his eye and comes over)*. Two rare steaks and salad please, with a bottle of your house red wine. Thank you. *(The bar lady takes* *the order, smiles, takes the menus and goes).* The Spirit. *(Pause).* Something else for you to remember. *(Smiles at Boy).* All three types of energy have a particular way of being *(pause)* gathered up, let's say, by the humans. Feeling energy is gathered when they are aware of and showing 'who they are' in their day to day life. The energy they find will be a 'plus' or 'minus' score depending on the corresponding Power Needs of the person. *(Significantly).* The spiritual type of energy is sourced by the human beings in a completely different way…

Boy: *(The bar lady returns with glasses and wine and starts to uncork the bottle).* Really. How interesting.

Prospero: And this is how. Please remember or maybe you could even record this with your phone. *(Boy starts to fiddle with his mobile phone whilst the bar lady prepares to pour the wine for tasting).* The human being finds and connects to the spiritual energy by performing rituals and using prayer or meditations which are meaningful, relevant and personal to each of them as unique individuals. *(Prospero sniffs and tries the wine, making grand gestures as he does so).* Exquisite. We shall have the rest.....

Boy: *(Still fiddling with his phone).* Got it now......

Prospero: *(The bar lady leaves and Prospero gives his full attention to Boy).* The more regularly a person gathers up this type of energy, the better they become at doing so. In the past, human beings were very aware of this fact, and would often practice their rituals. It was an important duty for them.

Boy: *(Points the phone at Prospero as if he was interviewing him).* Testing...Testing.... And why was this?

Prospero: *(Slightly louder and into the phone).* Partly because it was acknowledged amongst the human beings that it was a good idea to top up on the feeling energy levels every now and then, because it was impossible to predict when this feeling energy level might drop. Anything could happen and it often did. If daily events became difficult, levels would start to fall. *(He is becoming slightly far away from the mobile phone for recording purposes and Boy mimes to him to come a bit closer. He does so with a scowl on his face).* And partly because the human beings needed a fully set up, 100% guaranteed connection, ready to go into the spiritual energy source, because if and when they needed to sustain themselves by switching to this type of energy, they were able to do so straight away.

Boy: Right! Well, that makes sense. *(Said into the mobile phone).* Tell me Prospero. What on earth does the third method of gathering up energy involve then?

Prospero: Well, this is where it all gets very interesting, Boy. *(Grabs the phone off him and holds it in front of his mouth so he can now talk comfortably and still look at Boy).*

Boy: *(Boy stares at him).* Well, do tell me.

Prospero: *(Who is not comfortable with the mobile phone recording. He turns the phone off and puts it on the table).* I will get there eventually. I need to continue by telling you more human being history. *(Smirks).* Where is this food?

Boy*: (Settling into his chair).* I'm right with you.

Prospero*:* So. To recap. *(Fiddling with his napkin).* Human beings lived as I have been describing, for centuries. Gathering up feeling energy as the standard method, and with brief toppings up of spiritual energy everyday, so keeping the connection to the spiritual source of energy open in case of an emergency. This meant that the balance of feeling and spiritual energy sourced was pretty consistent. *(He stretches).* I would guess, as a rough guide, Boy, that most human beings in this time period would be gathering about 80% of their energy from the feeling method and approximately 20% from the spiritual. *(Pause).* However, as time passed by, the human species continued to evolve and big changes to this original energy balance started to emerge.

Boy: *(Playing with his cutlery).* Doesn't this usually happen to every species?

Prospero: *(Banging his wine glass).* No! Changes to the way energy is sourced? No way. But listen. No need to record me. *(Boy starts fiddling with his phone).* Just pay attention. Now then, there were two massive changes in the human being's culture during this time period, and these two changes caused the shift.

Boy: Go on…

Prospero: *(Prospero uses cutlery to move around and illustrate the points as follows).* The first change was this. The human beings started to develop an interface between themselves and their spiritual energy connection. They called this Religion, Boy. And different groups of human beings started to make up different sorts of religion.

Boy: *(Looking with surprise at the salt cellar that Prospero was using to symbolise Religion)* Really! An interface? What did they need an interface for?

Prospero: *(Sighs).* Because Boy, and I know this sounds ridiculous to you but please, see if you can understand. The people developed a need to try and work out what the spiritual energy was, where it came from, and to, well, how can I put it nicely. They had to sort of, well, make it relevant to themselves. They wanted to make the spiritual energy all about them. They couldn't see; or if they could see, they had forgotten somehow, that they were mere moments of creation by something which they could never comprehend. *(Having a moment of inspiration).* They had forgotten that they were merely 'things' upon a table, Boy. *(Sternly and with disbelief).* They didn't even know that there was a table! Such fools. They thought that everything was to do with them; they didn't see that they were just silly little things like this salt and pepper pot on top of the table, sitting in the huge quantum existence of the universal restaurant. *(Prospero puts the salt cellar and cutlery back in the right place).* They decided somehow that they were the point of everything. So, they made up the notion of Religion to make this ridiculous idea true. *(Pause).*

Boy*: (Slightly stunned).* These human beings sure like to make things up, don't they?

Prospero*: (Carrying on regardless).* You see, the human being is an extremely arrogant animal, Boy. Is that the right word? Maybe ignorant is a better one. *(Prospero shakes his head).* No matter. *(Leans back in his chair and shrugs).* Some of these people probably wanted to make the spiritual energy something that they could understand and maybe even use for their own ends. I don't know. But whatever the reason, it meant that they started to define what this type of energy was, made rules up about it and so on and so forth. *(Pause).* Some societies even nominated particular people as being better at and having more knowledge about these Religions than anyone else. All of society had to listen to and adhere to these rules as set out by these leaders. Or else... *(Pause).* However, why Religion developed is not relevant to our discourse, so I shall not go into anymore detail. *(Shudders, takes* *his wine glass and sniffs his wine).* That's better……

Boy*:* Of course not. How dreadful these human beings can be!

Prospero*:* Absolutely, dear Boy. *(Drinks from his glass).* And here is our meal. Thank you. *(The bar lady gives the men their meal, makes sure they are happy, and then leaves them).* We are not going to spend any more precious time contemplating this ludicrous way of thinking. *(Looks at his meal, picks up his cutlery and starts eating with relish. Boy watches him, and then starts eating his own meal).* However, Religion is hugely relevant to the human being energy crisis because the Religion notion had an extremely significant effect on how well the people were able to gather up spiritual energy. This is what makes it so important. Listen. *(He stops eating to make his point).* The effect this Religion nonsense had on the human beings, was to make connection to the spiritual type of energy much, much harder for them.

Boy: Really? Oh my goodness. *(Stops eating too)*. How?

Prospero: Because the focus had changed. The actual method used to connect to the spiritual energy, had itself become the focus. The Religion, the new methodologies, definitions, rules, leaders, the whole lot, all became much more important than the actual connection with the energy source itself.

Boy: Are you sure about this? *(Disbelieving)*.

Prospero: *(Sternly)*. Well, that is the fact of the matter.

Boy: Sorry, Sir. I just think that this is the most alarming fact you have told me so far about these human beings.

Prospero: Well, it gets much worse Boy. Calm down and have some more wine. *(He pours some into Boy's glass)*. This is just the beginning.

Boy: *(Obviously slightly distrait)*. I mean, what on earth were they thinking?

Prospero: It is extremely foolish and has led to tragic results as you will see later. *(Pours more wine into his own glass and carries on eating).*

Boy: *(Still not eating. Earnestly, with increasing passion).* So, let me check that I have understood you correctly, Sir. The human beings created Religion. This meant that the spiritual method of gathering up energy was put into jeopardy. *(Pause. Tries again).* The human beings started to lose the ability to connect with 20% of their energy input because they started to follow Religion, which focused on the method of connection, rather than the actual source of the energy. The human beings didn't understand the nature of spiritual energy. To follow a Religion became the end result in itself, rather than a method of connection to the essential spiritual energy…….

Prospero: Yes. Very good. No notes either. Come on then, Boy, eat up. *(Boy reluctantly picks up his knife and fork).*

Boy: *(Distressed).* But tell me. Why. Why did following a Religion mean that the spiritual energy was harder to access?

Prospero*: (Eating slowly).* Now, concentrate, Boy. *(Slowly).* The leader human beings created man made rules and rituals. This meant, as time passed and generations of people lived and died, the people eventually believed that the only way they could access the spiritual energy was through following a Religion. The old knowledge that the point was to gather up actual spiritual energy and any human being could do this on their own terms, had been lost over time. The people had been told by the religious leaders that it was wrong to try and access spiritual energy in any other form except for the one they allowed. *(Pause).* For some people this didn't make a big difference to their energy state. They could still connect through the method of the Religion and so gather up good spiritual energy. For these people, Religion resonated with their own personal needs and development, so the rituals, prayers and mediations of their Religion had relevant meaning. But this was unusual, Boy. For most people, Religion became 'follow the leader', doing what they were told to do, and believing in a strict ideology. *(Pause).* These people were not choosing to engage with the Religion because it had a personal meaning, a connectedness to the energy of the universe. No, indeed. They were engaging with the Religion because that is what they were expected to do and what everyone else did. *(Pauses to eat).* And if, as a person living in a particular society, the rules and ideas associated with the local Religion conflicted with 'who you were', your essence, then you were led to believe that you couldn't access any of this energy at all, that you were not worthy or even perhaps a bad or evil person.

Boy: Yes, I can see this. *(Both still eating slowly).*

Prospero: *(Drinks some wine).* As time moved forward, some of the leader human beings started to tweak the rules of the Religions too. They started to use Religion to control people. Religion became so mixed up with the day to day concerns of politics, and by the way, before you ask; whether this was by design or coincidence is not the point. *(Pauses for a drink of wine).* The human beings gradually turned the process of gathering spiritual energy into an intellectual thought process which had an additional social control function as a bonus. In short, Boy, what Religion did was to put a block between you as an individual, and the gathering up of spiritual energy. It became socially unacceptable to gather spiritual energy for yourself. The only approved method of gathering up this energy was by following Religion. And this meant that you also had to follow the rules of society and behave appropriately. Or you may well be cast out! *(Finishes his wine with a flourish).*

Boy*: Dreadful. (Stops eating and pauses for a drink too).* The original knowledge of knowing that spiritual energy was a profound need for the human beings and not just an intellectual thought process. Totally lost and disregarded.

Prospero*: Indeed. (Starts to eat, finishing off his meal).* Access to spiritual energy is extremely important to the human being as individuals and also as a species. It is a fundamental need, and for them to have meddled with this energy relationship without having had any understanding of it, is pure insanity. *(Leans over the table and whispers).* It's one of the core reasons that the whole of the future of the human being as a species has been put into jeopardy.

Boy: Oh dear....

Prospero: *(Finishing his meal, as has Boy. He calls the bar lady over who sees him and comes to the table to take away the empty plates).* There you go, Boy, Religion, to coin a popular human phrase....is 'bad for the soul'. *(Prospero chuckles. Bar lady waits to see if the men want to order anything else).* Two coffees, please. *(Bar lady smiles and leaves).* Right, that topic is finished for now. *(Plays with napkin).* This was the first shift, Boy, which happened thousands of years ago and caused huge difficulties for the human beings regarding sourcing spiritual energy. The second shift was more recent. In the early 1900s in fact.

Boy: Nearly 100 years ago. That's not long ago is it. Can I record this please?

Prospero: Indeed, it is not. If you must, give it here. *(Prospero fiddles with Boy's phone and puts it on the table in front of him).* So, let's see. Where are we? Around the 1940s on earth. By now, most people in this Western society do not access spiritual energy very much at all. They are forgetting more and more. They are feeling much less peaceful in themselves. But, Boy, they do not realise. They are not aware.

Boy: Really?

Prospero: They have not a clue. No clue at all. *(Shakes his head).* They start to blame everything else that they can think of to explain the way they feel. Politics, the neighbours, the wife. Anything! But no matter. This is what it was like. *(Dramatically).* But then, suddenly Boy, out of nowhere, something extraordinary happened…

Boy: *(The coffee arrives and the bar lady serves the two men).* And what was that?

Prospero: The human beings suddenly stopped being 'who they were'.

Boy: They did what!

Prospero: *(The bar lady leaves their table).* The people stopped being 'who they were', Boy.

Boy: But that's impossible. They can't do that. 'Who they are' is their essence! That's what makes them a uniquely created human being.

Prospero: *(Sorting out the coffee with milk, sugar etc).* Yes, I know. And I agree.

Boy: *(Quite distraught).* You can't agree to what I just said. If they are not 'who they are', the person, the people, can't exist. They can't stop being a person. Because they are a person!

Prospero: *(Calmly).* I can agree with what you said. It is true what you say. It is impossible to be a uniquely created human being without being 'who you are'.

Boy: Well, I don't understand then. I am literally speechless. What happened? Did the species end? *(Whispering)*. It can't have done because there are human beings here…

Prospero: Here's your coffee. I will tell you. *(He gives Boy his coffee, sips his own and continues speaking quite calmly and softly).* Back to the 1900s. Society was changing again. Scientific advances had led to the creation of machines, the idea of education for everyone was born, politics became the working man's concern…….

Boy: *(Interrupting and whispering).* In the history books, Prospero, this is all seen as progressive, as beneficial.

Prospero: *(Frowning).* Like Religion Boy, machines, education, politics, whatever you may say, are not all inherently 'good' or 'bad' in themselves. They are all just ideas. What is 'good' and 'bad' is how they are implemented. But it doesn't look pretty, I agree. Anyway, let me carry on…

Boy: Yes, Sir. Sorry to interrupt. *(They both sip their coffee).*

Prospero: Machines and education changed the relationship the human beings had developed with each other, forever. This relationship had been changing for over 500 years, but the most recent ideas and inventions really did finish off the old way of living. People stopped looking after each other, stopped making everything they needed together and stopped finding food and produce for each other. They became pretty much independent of each other. A different type of society started to evolve. Nearly all the interdependency between the people had disappeared.

Boy: So how did the houses get built? How were the children looked after? How was food found?

Prospero: Hold it there. *(Looks sadly at Boy).* Another thing you need to know. Over a thousand years ago the human beings invented something called Money. Money, like Religion, is a huge subject. However, all we need to understand for now, is that in the 1900s, having Money meant that you could pay other people to provide the things for you, that before, years and years ago, the people that you lived with, in your social group, would have provided.

Boy: So, who would do these things for you now, then? Who would build your house?

Prospero: *(Laughing).* Well, anyone who had the skills that were needed to build the house.

Boy: And the same would go for looking after the children?

Prospero: Yes, indeed.

Boy: *(Puts his coffee down again).* Crikey! Anyone who had the skills could build your house or look after your children if you gave them Money to do it? Even if they didn't know or care about you? *(Prospero nods and sips his coffee. Boy looks horrified).* Incredible. *(Pause. He thinks).* So, how did the human beings get their Money?

Prospero*: Most of the people earnt Money by attending a school and staying in education and following a career, or leaving school, working with the machines and getting a job.

Boy*: (Thinking hard). So, the people would get Money by having a career or a job?

Prospero*: (Enjoying his coffee). Yes. And they would be doing this career or job every day.

Boy*: (Carefully, his coffee forgotten). The people would spend all day doing their career or jobs to get Money.

Prospero*: Yes. So, they could use the Money to pay for things that before they would either do themselves or do with other people in their social group. Or have done for them by another person in their small society.

Boy*: (Pause). So, let me check I have this right Prospero. I'm struggling again. People now, in the twentieth century, could pay anyone who had the skills, to do anything that they wanted them to.

Prospero: Yes. They would pay someone else who had a career or job in providing whatever it was that they wanted…

Boy: And they did not know the person that they were paying?

Prospero: Goodness me, Boy, of course not! Have you been paying attention? *(Puts his coffee down and scowls at Boy).*

Boy: *(Persevering).* So, they were giving people Money to people they didn't know, to do all the things that before, they either had to do for themselves, or that the society they lived in would provide for and with them……

Prospero: Precisely. Drink your coffee boy.

Boy: *(Automatically picks up his cup).* Even the things that people had to do in order to look after themselves.

Prospero: Yes. All the things that you either provided yourself or had provided for you by a fellow member of your group. *(Crossly).* Basically, Boy, nearly all the tasks and things that you need to do to make yourself safe, healthy and loved, were provided by strangers if you paid them. *(More kindly).* Have a mint, Boy. I know. It is shocking at first.

Boy: It certainly sounds odd Prospero. *(Changing the subject slightly).* Explain how this caused energy problems. I'm not sure I understand.

Prospero: *(Finishing his coffee and leaning back).* Right, this is where Power Needs come into our learning again. If a person doesn't directly do something, then even if they achieve the end result that they have decided upon, they can not create good feelings from it. It is impossible. The person may think that they have succeeded in completing a task, but they will not have good feelings about whatever it was. For example. If you build a house for yourself, you will feel good about this because you have actually physically built it. Paying Money to someone else to do this for you, is simply that. All you are actually doing is paying someone else Money to build a house for you. Simply paying or spending Money doesn't have a 'feel'. Why this is so, we will look at in more detail another time, but this is how it works.

Boy: *(Slowly).* So, the people are paying other people to do things. Things that if they did themselves, would have created a good feeling. Things that if they did themselves, would gather up some peaceful feeling energy.

Prospero: *(Nodding).* Yes. Exactly. But remember, although they don't do the work, so don't gather up any feeling energy from this activity, they do still have the end result, the house. But yes, well done. *(Leans back).* So, what do you think that means, Boy, from an energy point of view?

Boy: *(Puzzled).* Feeling energy cannot be created if you just pay someone Money to do something?

Prospero: Excellent! You are getting the hang of this. So once again, the Power Energy Store levels are reducing.

Boy: Oh dear….

Prospero: But very interestingly, at the same time, the human beings think that they are feeling good. Because they have paid a man to build a house, they do actually have a house to live in! The fact that they have created good feelings about this is, of course, not true. *(Smiling)*. We will save truth for another time.... *(Pause)*. But there is even worse news and another important point here. *(Smirks)*. Tell me, what are the people doing with their time? How are they spending their time, Boy?

Boy: *(Finally finishing his coffee)*. Hmmm... They are working in a career or a job?

Prospero: Yes. What for, Boy?

Boy: *(Quickly)*. To earn Money to pay other people, so that they can buy the goods and services from them that they want or need.

Prospero: Yes. *(Pause)*. So. The people are spending nearly all their time not being or doing what they would be doing if they had a freedom to express 'who they are'. They are instead working in either a career, based on what they studied, or working with a machine, in their job. And what for? Well, Boy, to earn Money.

Boy: *(Putting his cup down).* Wow! This is crazy stuff, Sir.

Prospero: *(Nodding).* We are nearly there. So, tell me. What effect would working to earn Money have on feeling energy levels? On the Power Energy Store?

Boy: Well, if feeling energy is accessed by being 'who you are' in your day to day life, and people are spending their time just working to get some Money, then the people will not be creating feeling energy. There are two reasons for this. Just spending Money is not doing anything in regards to Power Needs, so whatever you buy, it will not be gathered up as a feeling energy, and if a person has to behave or do actions that are nowhere near in line with 'who they are' in their career or job, then they are not creating any 'plus', or good feelings whilst they are working.

Prospero*: Very good. (Standing up to go. The bar lady approaches him).* Could I have the bill please? *(To Boy).* And don't forget, the people have also forgotten how to gather up energy using the spiritual method...

Boy*: (Standing up too).* So, is this what you meant when you said earlier that people suddenly stopped being 'who they are'?

Prospero*:* Yes. They stopped being 'who they are' and instead become whatever their career or jobs needed them to be... *(Looks around at the sky. The sunset is gone and the night is dark and cloudy).* Come along now, I think it may rain again....

Boy*:* Oh no....

Prospero*:* Oh yes. Put on your coat. *(He puts on his own coat and hands Boy his).* You could argue, Boy, that earning Money and having a job meant that the people stopped being 'who they were'. It caused them to stop being their own unique personal selves.

Boy: *(Puts his coat on).* So how on earth did the people carry on existing then? I thought 'who you were' was your essence?

Prospero: *(Turns to look at Boy, wrapped up in his coat).* And so it is. Their 'being', their essence, their 'who they are' was not killed, Boy. It was not killed, but merely squashed, forgotten, hidden. Stamped down by the boots of a society that told you that the accumulation of Money was the point of living......

Boy: *(Standing with Prospero, both with coats on, ready to leave).* The human beings were technically unique people. But in their day to day activities, in the physical existence of themselves, they were not.

Prospero: *(Starting to go).* After you, Boy. *(Boy starts to walk across Prospero towards the door).* Yes. Exactly. No sense of self. No feeling energy. Squashed essence. Terrible state, Boy. Energy crisis! Low feeling energy, cut off from the Power Energy Store. Too much grief, low or no way to access spiritual energy......

Boy: *(Shaking head).* Awful….

Prospero: Whole populations walking around with a Nothingness feeling……

Boy: *(Stopping and looking back at Prospero).* We're back where we started…

Prospero: *(Still standing where he was.)* Big, big crisis. Leaders panicking! How can they fix this? *(Puts up umbrella).*

Boy: *(Excited).* Create Somethingelseness! The Answer! Prospero!

Prospero: Yes, come on. It's pouring with rain. Save the species from societal suicide! What is it? Find the Answer….'Mind' energy!' *(Prospero pulls Boy under the umbrella and they dash out of the door).*

Blackout

Scene 2

A white box room with a wooden floor and high walls. There is a small square window very high up with the sun streaming through it. The sunbeam reaches the floor. In the middle of the room is a school desk, where Boy is sitting. There is a backboard on the wall opposite him. A small door behind him is shut. Prospero opens this door and marches into the room. He whisks passed Boy and stands in front of him, by the blackboard. He is wearing a cape and a mortas board hat.

Prospero: Morning, hey ho! *(Looks around and sees Boy).* The lesson today is all about 'mind' energy. We will begin by learning the basic principles of the Energy Dynamic model.

Boy: *(Putting a pencil, note pad and other study aids onto his desk).* The Energy Dynamic model, Sir?

Prospero: Indeed, yes. It is a framework, designed over a period of 25 years in a place called Britain, around about the year 2000. It looks at *(writes this on the board).* The way human beings use energy. *(Turns around to look at Boy).* We're going to use this theory to help us to understand how 'mind' energy works. Is this clear, Boy?

Boy: *(Scribbling in his notepad).* Yes, Sir.

Prospero: The Energy Dynamic model uses an imaginary construct that can define and describe the abstract natures of the different ways human beings access energy. This allows us to see, explain and understand the ways particular human beings behave. This model allows us to work out any person's particular energy pattern, or Energy Dynamic.

Boy: Will the human beings be able to use and understand this, too?

Prospero: *(Chuckles).* The model has been developed specifically for the people. The whole purpose of it is so that they can start to understand what they are actually doing to themselves.

Boy: I can't wait!

Prospero: Good. So, Boy, take down notes. We have already looked at Laws 1 and 2. So, we can start with Law number 3 today. *(Writes this on the board).*

LAW 3

'YOU' ARE YOUR PERSONALITY, YOUR
PREFERENCES, YOUR ABILITY, YOUR
KNOWLEDGE, YOUR IQ, YOUR PHYSICAL
APPEARANCE, YOUR PHYSICAL BODY....
IN SHORT, 'YOU' ARE YOUR 'BRAIN'.

THE MOST FUNDAMENTAL PART OF THIS
'YOU', IS YOUR 'IMAGINATION'....

Prospero: *(Turns to look at Boy and starts to pace the floor).* This law is most interesting, Boy. Human beings have often debated what they actually are, what is it that makes them an individual person, unique and distinctive from everyone other person. But what actually does make one human being different to every other one? (*Paces the floor*). Well, here we have it! (*Pause*). 'You' are what your brain is and 'does'. (*Points to board*). And Boy, if you strip all the different pieces of this away, if you break the 'you' down to find the deepest part, Boy, if you strip all the layers of the 'you-ness' away, what you will ultimately end up with is the human being's imagination. Every other part of the 'you', Boy, can be changed, manipulated, or both, by outside events. (*Pause*). The parts of the 'you' that are affected in this way, can not possibly be the hard core nut part of 'you'! And if a replica of a part of a 'you' can be found in another person, then this must also mean that the part of 'you' that appears to be in someone else, can not therefore be, at the same time, the unique part of 'you'.

Boy*: (Listening hard). * Replica?

Prospero*:* It is perfectly possible, indeed even desirable, for the human beings to find the same part of themselves in someone else. I will give you some examples for us to discuss. (*Turns round and continues to write on the board*). Identical twins often have the same IQ and physical appearance. *(Scribbles on the board).* Someone's class, culture and education can mean that their preferences, hobbies and knowledge will be similar to another person from a similar background. How somebody was brought up, what their memories and life experiences have been, can shape them into being very similar to another person who has a shared past. *(Turns around again).* Human beings like this similarity, Boy, because it allows them to relate to each other's 'truth', or in other words, they experience this as a recognisable connection between themselves. *(Pause).* However, Boy, the imagination is different. The imagination can never be duplicated! The imagination is always unique. The human being's imagination, Boy, is what keeps him or her from imploding into the masses of everyone else's 'stuff'. It is where their unique essence lies, and is what makes them an individual. It is what keeps them firmly separate from everyone and everything else on this planet. By the human beings defining themselves as 'separate' beings from each other, they can experience 'separateness'! *(Pause).* And it is also the only way, paradoxically, that they can exist and be together. *(Boy looks puzzled, so Prospero tries again).* It is the uniqueness of the imagination that prevents the people from falling together into an oblivion of 'sameness', or 'togetherness'.

Boy*:* Hmmm….

Prospero*:* It is absolutely fascinating, Boy. Look. It is paradoxical. Let me draw this again. *(Turns to the board and starts scribbling).* Although the imagination separates the human beings from each other in an animal, physical way, it does, at the same time, connect each and everyone of them together. This is because of the nature of energy, because they are only able to gather up the feeling and spiritual energy by having a sense of their own uniqueness. They need this awareness to feed off the energy. They are able to connect to the universal energy because of, not despite of, their inherent acknowledgement of their uniqueness.

Boy*: (Looking at the board and his notes).* I'm not sure I understand.

Prospero: *(Sighs).* Simply put, the imagination has two functions. On the one hand, personal imagination separates and creates the human beings into different beings from each other. It is part of 'who they are', and it is also how they actually realise 'who they are'. Added to this, the imagination, the awareness of the fact that they are separate human beings created in a unique form, is the essential component for gathering up the feeling and spiritual energy. *(Pause).* How else can the human beings manifest 'who they are' in their day to day lives, if they have no imagination with which to be aware of and show this fact?

Boy: *(Slowly).* I see……

Prospero: *(Getting slightly excited).* Once they are aware of their uniqueness, start to acknowledge and value the fact that they are specially made creations, they can start to make good choices in their day to day lives. Being 'who they are' becomes a good experience for them. Or in other words, Power Needs say yes! 'Plus' feelings are created! The person starts to hoover up large amounts of feeling energy, just by being themselves. And this feeling energy not only creates peace, but also acts like a glue that joins everyone up. They are all feeling energy gatherers! They are all connecting in the same way. *(Clears his throat. Calms down. Pause).* For now, though, Boy, just realise that the imagination both separates and defines, as well as joins up and connects.

Boy: *(Not sure).* Right, then. I see. *(Assertively).* So, it is a very important part of the human being's makeup.

Prospero: Indeed, it is absolutely essential for their existence. *(Sits down at his desk).* However, yet again, Boy, the human beings, of course, have no clue whatsoever that the imagination is what makes them the unique creations that they really are. Which, of course, causes them huge problems. But I digress, Boy. (Gets up and turns back to the board). The important point here as regards the Energy Dynamic model, is to understand what makes up the 'you' part of a person.

Boy: I have that now, Prospero.

Prospero: Good. So, now we are ready for Law number 4. *(He rubs out all the writing on the board and starts afresh).*

LAW 4

YOUR 'MIND' IS SEPARATE FROM YOUR 'BRAIN'.

'EMOTION' IS CREATED IN THE 'MIND' AND IS NOTHING TO DO WITH WHAT 'YOU' 'FEEL'.

Prospero: *(Turns round and faces his 'class').* Now then. The second point. It is fundamental to the model that we understand that what people feel, is completely different to what is commonly called emotion. Let me help you here. *(On the board).* 'Feel' is to do with feeling energy and is to do with how you experience being 'who you are' in day to day life. This can be a 'plus' feeling or a 'minus' feeling. Peace or Grief. Emotion is completely different. It is to do with the mind and is based on the mind reaction to what is happening around you. Are you following? *(Turns around).*

Boy: *(Scribbling notes).* Well, I'm a bit confused, really. Don't the human beings think that feeling and emotion are the same thing? I'm sure they do. And how can it be said that the mind is different to the brain?

Prospero: *(Starting to pace again).* Let us pause here whilst we consider detail and revision. Remember, what you feel is to do with how much a situation allows you to be 'who you are', and this is assessed by your brain, which calculates what your Power Need score is, in any given situation. Generally speaking, the more you are able to 'be you' in a situation, the more your Power Need score will increase and the higher your feeling energy score will be.

Boy: I remember Prospero. But you need to tell me what these Power Needs are. Now.

Prospero: Here you go then; the time is right. Law number 5. *(He reads this out from a notebook and flings it on Boy's desk when he has finished).*

LAW 5

POWER NEEDS ARE USED TO WORK OUT WHAT 'YOU'
'FEEL' IN YOUR DAY TO DAY LIFE ACTIVITIES.
IF ALL YOUR POWER NEEDS ARE BEING FULFILLED IN A
SITUATION, GIVEN 'WHO YOU ARE', THEN 'YOU' WILL
SCORE A ZERO OR PLUS 'FEEL' SCORE.
IF THEY ARE NOT FULFILLED, GIVEN 'WHO YOU ARE' THEN
'YOU' WILL SCORE A MINUS 'FEEL' SCORE.

THERE ARE 10 DIFFERENT POWER NEEDS.
EACH POWER NEED HAS ITS OWN SCORE IN A SITUATION.
THEIR TOTAL IS CALLED THE 'FEEL SCORE'.

THERE ARE FOUR DIFFERENT TYPES OF 'POWER NEEDS'.
THESE ARE THE 'ANIMAL' POWER NEEDS (SAFETY,
HEALTH, LOVE/CARE), 'HUMAN' POWER NEEDS (BELONGING,
IDENTITY, MEANING, PURPOSE) 'PERSONALITY' POWER
NEEDS (LEARNING STYLE, EXPRESSION OF SELF), AND
'ABILITY' POWER NEEDS (ABILITY).

'ANIMAL' POWER NEEDS HAVE THE HIGHEST RATING; THE
'ABILITY' POWER NEED IS THE LOWEST RATING.
ONE 'FEEL SCORE' FROM AN 'ANIMAL' POWER NEED IS
WORTH ABOUT 5 TIMES MORE THAN ONE 'FEEL SCORE'
FROM AN 'ABILITY' POWER NEED

YOUR 'FEEL SCORES' (HOW YOU HAVE 'FELT' IN ALL THE
SITUATIONS IN YOUR LIFE) ARE KEPT IN YOUR 'BEING
YOU' ENERGY STORE.

Boy: *(Looking at the notebook).* Thank you. So now I know. *(Pause).* Tell me, how does the brain work out what the 'feel score' is in each situation? And what is the 'Being You' energy store?

Prospero*:* The 'Being You' energy store is the old name for the Power Energy Store. So just mentally replace the modern name for the old one instead. Detail on the 'feel score' is as follows. The brain looks at the facts of the situation. An example. *(Writes on the board).* 'I am walking in the park and it is a sunny day'. The brain takes these facts and then works out what happens to the different Power Needs given these facts. Your total 'feel score' could be a zero or above, (which is a 'plus feel'), or below zero (a 'minus feel').

Boy*:* I understand the principle. Great. Could you tell me more about these Power Needs?

Prospero*:* We look at all of this in the Power section of our learning. For today, we need to understand Law 4 before we look at Law 5 properly. You must understand what happens within the human dynamic of mind, brain, emotion and feel first. Now then, listen. *(Pause. Pacing).* When the brain calculates what all the Power Need scores are for a specific situation, the separate scores are added up to give the total; the 'feel score'. *(Stops and looks around).* This is what you are feeling. And this information, along with the facts of the situation that you are in at the time, are sent to your mind to process…

Boy*:* Right, so the mind processes what the brain has calculated. And the brain has calculated your 'feel score' in the given situation. This sounds fairly simple, Right, so, the next obvious question is, how does the mind do this?

Prospero*:* Ahhhh, what a question, Boy. *(Leans against his desk and looks into the distance).* Well. Let's see. The mind is part of the brain. It is a small part of the brain. *(Pause).* The easiest way to explain the mind is to look at its function. *(Pacing).* Pretend that it is an office. It is the Head Quarters of the person, Boy. And in this 'mind office' lives an administrative assistant whom we can call 'Admin'. Admin's job is to make sure that all the information sent to the office by the brain, all the information about what is going on in reality, about how the person feels about what is happening, so on and so forth, is processed.

Boy: *(Looking doubtful).* I see.

Prospero: *(Pacing around the room).* The 'mind office' as a processor of information is very effective, because it means that the brain is free to gather up new information as it happens. The job of the brain is to gather up the facts and feelings as life passes by. The 'mind office' only stores the information and keeps things ordered and neatly filed. *(Back to the board).* For example, all the information is stored on a database, Boy, and this could be called a person's memory.

Boy: *(Busy scribbling).* Yes, I understand......

Prospero: *(Starts pacing again).* However, Boy, this is what is supposed to happen. But often it does not. Human beings malfunctioning again.

Boy: No!...

Prospero: *(Getting overexcited again).* When a person is cut off by the brain from the

Power Energy Store, the 'mind office' stops merely processing and storing information, and instead becomes the person's decision maker! The brain has detected too much grief in the Power Energy Store and so tells the mind, or in other words, 'Admin', to take control and to try to keep the person out of trouble. *(Dramatically, over Boy).* Admin takes this very seriously. Admin starts to make decisions! *(Pause).* Admin only has access to information as it is sent to him, he has no idea about what is actually happening, he can't see outside his office, so he just guesses what might be happening by looking at the past events that he has stored in his office. Chaos comes to town. *(Starts pacing).* The conclusions that Admin comes to when he makes his decisions about what the person must do next, are based purely on the paperwork that Admin has lying around in the office. All from the past. *(Standing over Boy's desk again).* Of course, this often has nothing to do with what is actually happening in the present moment! *(Turns away and addresses the room).* In other words, Boy, an Admin officer has just become the boss and he hasn't got a clue. *(Sarcastically).* But never mind about this detail! As soon as Admin has made his decision, he communicates this to the person directly. And he does this by pressing emotion buttons. Admin uses emotion to communicate. Emotion is purely and simply Admin's way of letting you know what he thinks you must do. Oh, and if you have a clever admin, he might try shouting at you first before he blasts you out of the blue with a terrifying emotion!

Boy*: (Horrified again).* Shouting!

Prospero*:* Yes, this will be experienced as an inner thought or 'voice in the head'. Humans can find this most alarming. *(Wraps his cape around him in a dramatic manner).*

Boy*: (Amazed at the performance).* Really. How fascinatingly illogical Sir. What a horrible set up…

Prospero*: (In his stride).* It is indeed, but only because Admin is being forced by the brain to take control, and using the emotion buttons and shouting are the only things he has to use. Poor Admin. Suddenly in charge. But what a silly human being! I mean, its terribly obvious isn't it, Boy. It is absolutely as clear as day to see the solution. I mean, Boy, all they have to do is…Are you following me, Boy? Boy….!

A loud bell starts ringing and a voice off stage crying out 'next class please'. Boy hurriedly grabs his items and leaves Prospero standing there.

Blackout.

Scene 3

The same as Scene 2 but Prospero is sitting at his desk and Boy comes into the room and sits down on his chair. A bell rings.

Prospero: *(Writing notes at his desk).* Good. We are making excellent progress. I think it is time now for us to put the two topics that we have been discussing, together. *(Looks up).* How about it?

Boy: *(Settling down).* Yes, Sir. Whatever you want.

Prospero: *(Getting up and moving towards a projector).* Now, remember what we learnt about energy last time, Boy. Feeling energy. Here is a description for you. This is how a human being might experience it in their day to day life… *(He turns on the projector and these words appear on the wall…He reads them out).*

'BEING YOU' 'ENERGY STORE' — WHERE ALL THE 'FEELS' IN YOUR LIFE ARE STORED.

IF YOU ARE 'FEEDING OFF' YOUR 'BEING YOU' ENERGY YOUR GENERAL EXPERIENCE OF LIFE WILL BE LIKE THIS:

ABSOLUTE: YOU WILL ALWAYS 'FEEL' THE SAME. IT DOESN'T REALLY MATTER WHAT YOUR THOUGHTS ARE, OR WHAT HAPPENS IN THE DAY-TO-DAY.

CALM: WHEN YOU HAVE TO MAKE DECISIONS YOU 'KNOW' WHAT TO DO; THE 'FACTS' ARE OBVIOUS, YOU KNOW WHAT YOU 'FEEL' ABOUT THEM (PLUS OR MINUS 'FEEL' SCORE). YOU DO NOT NEED TO GUESS OR RATIONALISE ABOUT THINGS FOREVER.......

PERMANENT: YOU FEEL PEACEFUL (OR SAD) AS A CONTINUAL BACKGROUND 'HUM' DURING YOUR DAY-TO-DAY EVENTS, WHATEVER THEY MAY BE.

QUIET: YOU EXPERIENCE THE 'BEING YOU' ENERGY AS PEACEFULNESS (OR GRIEF). THIS IS NOT AN EMOTIONAL STATE AND IS MISSED IF YOU ARE NOT WHOLLY CONNECTED TO YOUR 'BEING YOU' ENERGY STORE, AND WILL DEFINITELY BE DROWNED OUT IF YOU BECOME EMOTIONAL.

LAW 6B

BEING YOU ENERGY HAS GOT NOTHING TO DO WITH
'DOING WELL' IN A DAY TO DAY EVENT......

BEING YOU ENERGY COMES FROM THE KNOWLEDGE
THAT 'YOU'.......

- ARE IN A GOOD SAFE SPACE ('PLUS' POWER
  NEEDS)
- BEING 'YOURSELF' ('WHO YOU ARE')

Prospero*: (Turns around and sadly speaks to class).* That is how the human beings lived for many many years, until they started to feel Nothingness, and the leaders came up with the Answer... Any questions? *(Starts pacing around the classroom).* Now, Boy, I would like to go back to the discussion we had in the restaurant. We finished at the point where the human beings were desperate. Suffering from a Nothingness. Cut off by the brain from their Power Energy Store. Full of grief. The people had stopped being 'who they were' and could not access feeling energy. Meanwhile, they had forgotten about the spiritual method of gathering up energy as well. Dangerous times! *(Pause).* However, the leaders of the people had come up with an Answer. This

Answer meant accessing energy in a new way. Mind energy is created! *(Pause).* The people believed in this Answer and started to focus on getting as much energy as they could by using this method. Here are the laws regarding this type of energy.

Law 7b

IF YOU ARE FEEDING OF YOUR 'MIND' ENERGY, YOU GENERAL EXPERIENCE OF LIFE WILL BE LIKE THIS....

RELATIVE – YOU WILL SEE THINGS AND ENJOY THEM OR NOT DEPENDING ON HOW WELL YOU DID THEM BEFORE AND USUALLY ON HOW WELL YOU THINK YOU SHOULD DO...

ADDICTIVE – YOU WILL NEED TO TOP UP ON 'MIND' ENERGY EVERY DAY AND THE 'TICK' OR 'CROSS' IS EXPERIENCED AS A 'ONE OFF' EMOTIONAL HIT...

EXHAUSTING – AS THIS ENERGY IS GATHERED UP BY DOING SOMETHING AT THE SAME OR A HIGHER STANDARD THAN YOU DID THE LAST TIME, YOU NEED TO KEEP 'ACHIEVING' MORE AND MORE, OR FINDING 'NEW' THINGS TO DO, TO ENSURE THAT YOU CAN KEEP FINDING 'TICKS'..

NOTICEABLE – IT IS EASY TO TELL WHEN YOU ARE EXPERIENCING AN EMOTION! IF YOU ARE SCORING MORE 'TICKS' THAN 'CROSSES' YOU WILL BE HAVING MAINLY POSITIVE EMOTIONS. SCORING 'CROSSES' WILL MEAN THAT YOU WILL BE EXPERIENCING NEGATIVE EMOTIONS.

'MIND' ENERGY IS GATHERED UP BY HOW YOU 'DO' IN YOUR DAY-TO-DAY EVENTS.

Law 8

'REAL WORLD' – WHAT IS ACTUALLY HAPPENING AROUND YOU. THIS MUST BE IN THE PRESENT AND FACTUAL. IT IS WORKED OUT BY THE BRAIN.

Boy: *(Looking pleased).* Understood Prospero.

Prospero: *(Summing up).* The laws we have just looked at describe the experiences people have when they live off the different types of energy.

Boy: Great. *(Looks back at notes).* I'm not so sure about this 'Being You' energy, the old way of describing the Power Energy Store. Can you explain a bit more please?

Prospero: This is where your feelings are kept. *(Pause).* Let me give you an example. If you have been mainly in situations where, when you have been 'who you are' during your life, you have scored 'plus' feeling experiences, then we could safely predict that your Power Energy Store would be in good shape and that you would experience this as contentment. However, if you suddenly became cut off from this energy for whatever reason, you would not only lose connection to your Power Energy Store, but would also be unable to access any more energy from the feeling method. So, in order to find some energy to live off, unless you were an expert at gathering up energy from the spiritual way, you would have to use the Answer, or the 'mind' method. Admin will be put in charge of energy collection. Every time you did well in a situation your Admin would notice and would give you an emotional positive experience. This is called scoring a 'tick'. You feed off this type of energy instead of feelings. *(Abrupt stop).* This is not a good situation, Boy.

Boy: *(Busy writing).* Tell me why….

Prospero: *(Pacing around the room again).* People, when living off their mind energy, are controlled by their Admin Assistant. This is because the brain has decided to give the mind complete control over the person. The person has created too many sad feelings. They are cut off. The person experiences this as losing all sense of being. The person disappears into the Nothingness zone. *(Quietly).* They experience 'nothing', and in effect this is true. They have been cut off from their feelings and can not show 'who they are'. The person has to turn to their mind for help. For identification. For a boundary. Who are they? What can they be?

They have forgotten their inherent self! They can't see the facts of the situation they are in and what they feel anymore! They must enter the realm of the 'mind'. They have no choice. They cannot survive in a state of Nothingness. *(Turns round in a sinister way).* And so, to help these poor, lost creatures, the mind, their new boss, Admin, creates them an illusion....

Boy: *(Startled).* My goodness! Why?

Prospero: *(Sternly).* The mind has to do this, it has to create an illusion. *(Pause).* It creates an illusion so that the person can think that they are all right. We are in survival mode remember, and the brain has to keep the person going somehow. *(Pause).* The brain hands over truth management to the mind, to Admin. Admin has got to get the person out of trouble. Admin has to gather up mind energy and find some 'ticks'. *(Pause).* For the process of this 'tick' collection to work, the person has to have some sort of definition, some sort of role *(earnestly)*. They have to, Boy; the person can not define themselves by 'who they are' anymore. They need something outside of them to give them a persona. A substitute 'who they are'! *(Pacing)*. It works too! Once the person has been taken over by the 'illusion', they often start to think that they are better. They start to enjoy 'collecting ticks'! Admin is pleased too, he has saved the day. He gives the person little buzzy emotional hits to keep them going. People start to think that how well they do or how badly they don't do each day, is a direct reflection of themselves. Can you believe all this! *(Shudders)*. They start to use words like 'winning' or 'losing'.

Boy: *(Suddenly)*. Like someone who has to hit a target and thinks that they are great when they succeed in it?

Prospero: *(Surprised)*. Yes, exactly like that. The mind energy they gather up is completely dependent on how well they do, or don't do, on a daily basis. If they do well, they score a 'tick'. If they do badly, they score a 'cross'.

Boy: *(Shaking his head)*. 'Tick collecting!'

Prospero: *(Defensively).* Well, Boy, they have to. This is the Answer they have been given and they have to believe in it! Because they are cut off from their feel and have forgotten about the spiritual method of connection, they are totally reliant on how successful they think their day has been. Success is a mind energy tick! The people have expectations and targets! They need to collect enough mind energy to keep on being motivated, Boy. They have been cut off from their 'feel' remember? They have no other energy source. If they don't achieve their targets, this is terrible news for them. Too many crosses! Severe anguish. Low mind energy means they think they are no good or useless. They won't know what to do with themselves.

Boy: Dear me, Sir. What happens then?

Prospero: They have to score some extra ticks to keep going. They project into the future. They start thinking about what they will do during the next day and how they can achieve their goals or targets. They start planning and thinking! Admin becomes reassured. Admin stops shouting at them.

Boy: They have to achieve all the time? To think and plan! Just to have enough mind energy to carry on! That sounds exhausting.

Prospero: *(Abruptly)*. It is very common in this world today. 'Tick collecting' is the Answer remember. People spend all their lives doing this. They are trained to 'tick collect'. It works. It only goes wrong when people fail to find 'ticks' and start to collect 'crosses' instead. But if that doesn't happen, they can go on forever like this. So. *(Turning his back to Boy)*. Is there anything else?

Boy: The Power Energy Store is where people keep their feeling energy. And this is to do with 'who they are' and their Power Needs.

Prospero: Yes. Day to day life affects a person all the time and creates 'plus' or 'minus' feelings for every situation, even if the person is not aware of this. These 'minus' feeling scores eventually end up in the Power

Energy Store as they are stored in the mind office when the person is cut off. As soon as the person re - connects to the Power Energy Store, the 'minus' feelings make their way into the feeling store. Imagine that the Power Store is like a glass bowl; the 'plus' feelings are like clear drops of water, the 'minus' feelings are like drops of ink.

Boy: *(Scribbling).* I will note that. Right. So, can I ask for an example?

Prospero: Certainly. Let's pretend 'who we are' does not like cats, it is our personal preference. If in our day to day life, cats suddenly start appearing, we will start scoring a 'minus' feeling every second for as long as that cat is there in our situation. There is nothing at all *(underlining this)* whatsoever, we can do to change this. If part of 'who we are' is 'I don't like cats' then we are going to have 'minus' feelings until the situation has no cats in it.

Boy: *(Thinking hard).* Even if we try and think we do like cats? Even if we think we should like cats and that it is us, just us being silly not liking them?

Prospero: Yes. *(Laughs).* Spoken like a true 'tick collector', Boy. 'Minus' feelings will still be created even if we manage to think that we do like cats. *(Pause).* If, according to ourselves, according to our brain's knowledge of 'who we are' and calculation of our Power Needs, if the truth is that we do not like cats, then we will have 'minus' feelings no matter how much we try and try to persuade ourselves that we do think cats are lovely fluffy beasts! *(Laughing).* We can try all we like to get around this fact, but the truth will remain.

Boy: So, what do people do if they do have an unwanted 'cat' in their life? What do they do if their actual day to day life is giving them 'minus' feeling scores but they need to have the cat there because they are 'tick collecting'? *(Horrified thought).* What if the very cat they don't like, is giving them a 'tick'?

Prospero: Ah ha, various peculiar things that I will explain later, but very interestingly, Boy, one of the most common ideas, or techniques, used today in these situations, and indeed is sold to the people as part of the Answer, is called *(dramatic pause)* 'Positive Thinking'. *(Loudly).* There is nothing positive about this at all. It is in fact, very sad! *(As if making a speech).* People who practice Positive Thinking do not believe in energy collection from feelings. They believe that a feeling is the same as an emotion. Therefore, they think that in order to feel better then they need to achieve in the day to day. They are addicts of 'tick collection'. They believe in the Answer. They have to gather up almost all their energy through 'ticks', but do not realise what they are doing. They believe the Answer is all there is, and that this is true.

Boy: My goodness me….

Prospero: *(Pacing).* They think that they feel better when they have success. Of course they do, because this achievement means that they score a 'tick', a positive mind energy hit. They emotionally experience a 'high'! When they do achieve something compared to the day before, or compared to someone else, or compared to something that they have decided is a target, they get a rush of this mind energy by way of an emotion, and think that they feel good. *(Pause).* However, we all know that a 'tick' has got nothing whatsoever to do with a feeling. *(Rambling slightly).* Mind energy fades after a day or so mainly because it is just a relative 'win' about something that is not really connected to 'you'. The win is connected to an event that is outside of 'you' and only exists during a moment of time. *(Pause).* Although very pleasant as an experience, Boy, this has actually nothing to do with 'who you are' in a fundamental way. The person will experience elation, adrenaline, a 'buzz', or whatever, but what these short, sharp 'highs' are actually doing is taking attention away from the fact that the person has a feeling of Nothingness, which is why they can not access any energy through the feeling way in the first place.

Boy: *(Sighing).* Give me a simple example, Sir.

Prospero: *(Still pacing).* It is similar to drinking an energy drink to keep you going. The truth is that you are absolutely exhausted because you need nourishment. But instead of stopping and building yourself up and eating something that will nurture you, you drink a high energy drink full of chemicals that will just make you think that you have more energy so you can carry on.

Boy: *(Nodding).* Thank you, Sir.

Prospero: *(Waving his arms around etc).* The Positive Thinkers do not understand this. They carry on achieving in their day to day events, because they genuinely think it works. They think that if you fail to achieve a goal or target, it's because you are not trying or being focused enough. They believe that you are doing something wrong. Scoring a 'cross' is seen as a weakness by these people and they believe that this weakness can be overcome by more Positive Thinking; by trying harder. *(Pause).* Boy, they refuse to see that the reason a person may not be achieving something is actually because they either don't want to achieve it, because it isn't 'who they are', or because they can't actually get to it, they actually haven't got enough energy in their Power Energy Store to make it.

Boy: Goodness me.

Prospero: To summarise, Boy, Positive Thinkers look to the outside world, their mind created illusion, to give them objects, activities or challenges which create 'ticks' for them. A positive response from another person from doing these things is a 'tick'. They can live off this mind energy they gather up and it is experienced by them as a very pleasant emotional reaction as they achieve these positive responses.

Boy: Really?

Prospero: *(Exasperated).* They love the Answer, Boy. Its habit, they have always known it. It's the culture they live in. They are told it works. Everyone else believes in it! They think that if they feel sad, they just need to score more 'ticks'. *(Sarcastically).* Then they don't feel sad anymore! And if they do feel sad, then there must be something wrong with them. *(Pause. Turns to Boy).*

When a lot of people think something works, other people believe them. People like having the Answer. The leaders who encourage this behaviour are very good at showing others that it does work. They preach about it by saying that Positive Thinking can beat any blockage for a start. That the mind is the most powerful element of a human being. They absolutely and faithfully preach that this is truth.

Boy: Sounds....

Prospero: *(Pacing around the room impatiently).* I haven't finished yet. People don't know about feeling energy anymore, so they need to be looking out for something else that keeps them going because they are pretty much cut off all the time. Logically and rationally, the truth is, and this is extremely significant Boy, the truth is this. *(With passion).* If a person has to even consider thinking about motivating themselves by Positive Thinking about something in the first place, then they obviously don't want to do it, do they? If they did want to do it, they would just do it! Without having to motivate themselves or trying to do it! If you ever need to go into your mind to try and make yourself do something, then Boy, the truth is that you don't actually want to do it in the first place. *(Shouting)*. And do you know why, Boy? Do you know why a lot of people don't want to do what they think that they should be doing?

Boy: No.

Prospero: *(Getting louder)*. People don't want to do whatever it is because they actually don't literally, 'feel' like doing it. Because it will make them score 'minus' feelings!

Boy: Yes, well, that is quite frankly fairly obvious, Prospero.

Prospero: *(Almost despairing)*. But the people aren't aware of this, Boy! Or if they are aware they will not admit it! *(Sadly)*. They ignore the fact that they are carrying grief. They are completely oblivious and unaware of the fact, that if someone is struggling to achieve something, then there is probably something to do with the target or goal or with what they would have to do to achieve the target or goal, that is in fundamental conflict with 'who they are'.

Boy: *(Slightly alarmed at Prospero passion).* Right.

Prospero: *(Even louder).* Or, it could be that if the person simply can't summon up the energy to do whatever they need to do in order to achieve these things, then Boy, that person obviously does not have enough feeling energy to do it! It is too much for them!

Boy: Yes....

Prospero: *(Quieter).* The two main factors that make a person feel like not doing whatever it is that they are supposed to be achieving, are as follows. *(Almost whispering to Boy).* Because of the lifestyle the person has, their general Power Energy Store levels will be too low. And the 'who you are' aspect of the goal or target the person is trying to aim for will not be in line with their truth, their real self. These factors together will be having the same effect on the person as the unwanted cat has on the person who does not like cats.

(Quieter again). Receiving 'minus' feelings continuously, their essence...their 'who you are'....their 'brain'....their 'feelings'. *(In frustration, maybe banging a table).* They are all pointing to the fact that they don't really want to be there or do whatever it is!

Boy*:* Terrible!

Prospero*: (Turning round, with a flourish).* Positive Thinkers though, just say that you need to motivate yourself more, and why not try various tricks and techniques to help you.

Boy*:* How strange...

Prospero*: (Perches on desk).* One method employed by people who usually like to see themselves as successful, is to attempt to change the way their mind, or their Admin, reacts to 'minus' feelings. They tell Admin to stop looking at the feeling part of a life event. *(Pretends to shout at someone).* 'Look at something else!'. The Positive Thinker doesn't know this is what they are doing, because they don't believe in feelings in the first place. *(Shaking his head).* This 'looking at something else' chosen by the person to distract Admin, will be something that they will be able to get a few 'ticks' from and it will always make the day to day activity that they have to do, easier. These 'tick' collecting tasks are always to do with something that a person thinks will make things easier, rather than something that means you will make your world a better one from a feeling point of view.

Boy: *(Listening hard).* Example, Sir!

Prospero: *(Pacing, pause).* Buying a new car. If the person manages to achieve this, the goal will, in a day to day activity way, score them a 'tick'. They will have one tick in their mind energy store (because the person has achieved the target, by the way, not because they now have a new car). In the short term this means that their mind energy store is doing well. Think of mind energy as similar to a fire in a fire place in the office. A 'tick' is like a log of wood. This is how it works........

Boy: I'm concentrating.

Prospero*:* Admin needs the person to show that they are successful. The person listens to Admin. Admin is in charge. A new car will score a 'tick'! Admin tells the person this. The person is happy, they like a challenge in the illusion. It gives them a purpose, a meaning! However, it will be difficult, so the person wants some help to achieve this. They ask their Admin to keep them focused only on the 'car task', that's all. Admin does what he is told; he just wants the person to get on with it. Admin wants 'ticks'. *(Confidentially, as an aside).* He has been told by the brain that he is in charge of energy collection. Admin wants success! *(Back to normal).* So, Admin waits for the car 'tick'. He searches in the life events that arrive in the office for clues to do with 'buying a car'. *(Sits down).* When he does find one, he is happy. He can sit down and relax a bit. The hunt is going well! He will press an emotion button to show the person that he is pleased. The person receives a small emotional 'buzz'. Great news all around. *(Pauses, rolls eyes).* This will continue until the person actually does buy the car. When the 'car is bought' life event arrives in the mind office, the largest 'tick' has been found! There is a big 'tick' log of wood roaring in the fire! *(Gets up).* Both Admin and the person can have a rest. Admin will probably sit down and have a cup of tea, while the person runs around being excited. Admin has given him a big emotion buzz as a reward! *(Pause).* And all the 'minus' feeling scores that were gathered up whilst on the 'buying the car' hunt, will have not been noticed at all.

Boy: *(Nodding).* Very clever.

Prospero: *(Really being expressive).* So, Boy, can you see that over time this is an extremely destructive and damaging practice? It causes a huge build up of 'minus' feelings scores in your mind office. They are all ready to fall down into the Power Energy Store as soon as reconnection takes place. This is because the unwanted cat has always been there! Admin didn't notice. Your mind becomes, umm, well the best way to put it is, 'distorted'! Your Admin is only looking at the 'ticks' on the life events coming in. And you are telling him, sometimes even bullying him, to make sure that he does everything he can to help you achieve these 'ticks! *(Pointedly)*. No matter what is happening to you in your day to day life.

Boy*: That sounds worrying. Do people really do this?

Prospero*: (Sitting on his desk).* Oh yes, they do. They will do everything they possibly can do to ignore the fact that their 'sad feel' cat is sitting there right in front of them, so to speak. They will do anything to convince themselves and to trick their Admin into thinking that everything is fine, that the cat is not really there and that they feel rather good. They will surround themselves with the fruits of their 'ticks'. Their expensive cars, their high status jobs, anything they can achieve, anything they can win, just so that they can carry on collecting 'ticks', so that poor old Admin can keep the fire burning in the office. They will do anything to keep this going.

Boy*: Dreadful….

Prospero*: (Standing up and stretching).* I know. And the worst thing is, Boy, is that it is so easy to solve this whole energy crisis. The person only has to do one simple and most obvious thing.

Boy: Yes?

Prospero: *(Standing very still).* To acknowledge that the cat is there, that it is making them feel sad, and to slowly move away from it.

Boy: Is that all. Well, what stops them from doing this, Prospero?

Prospero: *(Looking for his coat, tidying up).* Fear, ignorance and weakness, Boy. Fear, because they think that they need their 'ticks' to survive and so will not risk losing even one. Ignorance, because they don't believe in the Power Energy Store or feeling energy. This fundamental ignorance means that it is very, very hard for them to move away from the cat, no matter how sad it makes them, because the person doesn't know about the different sorts of energy. So, they need to let the cat stay there in order to collect 'ticks'. To remove the cat from day to day life will probably mean destroying the illusion of success. You need a lot of power, Boy, to move away from your sad feeling cat. You need to be brave. You need to know who you are, what is going on and have a high Power Energy Store level. Most people are full of unacknowledged grief and hence, are very weak and dependent on the mind energy 'tick' collections.

Boy: *(A bit stunned).* So even if they could see it, even if they could see the cat, and even if they knew that it was creating sad feelings for them, they still wouldn't be able to move away from it.

Prospero: *(Putting his coat on).* Not as they are now, no, Boy. Not as they are now. But they could, Boy, anyone can start to build up their Power Energy Store. It's what people are here for. To be themselves. *(Shakes his head).* 'Ticks' are only a reaction to grief in the Power Energy Store, that's all. 'Ticks' become a bonus once there is no need for the Answer. Once people learn how to create again, they do not need the Answer. They become their own Solution. 'Ticks' become

'Frillies'; extra bonuses for creating 'plus' feelings in daily life. Creating 'plus' feelings by owning 'who they are' and making the world a better place. Choosing love, the most fundamental Power Need, over success, the illusion that makes the Answer real. Boy, people are their own Solution. As soon as they understand this, the Answer loses it hold....

Boy*:* There is hope then, Prospero, there is hope for the human species?

Prospero*:* *(Turns round with coat on, ready to go).* Oh yes, Boy. This is what we are here for. To show them. To show the people that they can start to have a strong Power Energy Store, not a grief weakness. People don't need to 'tick' collect if they can create good feelings. Slowly, slowly, they can rebuild their own Power Energy from within themselves. Come on, Boy. Time to go....

Boy*:* *(Getting ready too).* Sir, why aren't they all learning how to do this now? Immediately. Straight away.

Prospero: Because, my dear Boy, they must do something else first.

Boy: *(Slightly desperately)*. What? What do they have to do first?

Prospero: *(Pauses)*. They have to want to. They have to want to stop chasing 'ticks' in the illusion the Answer has created. They have to want to be less reliant on outside events. They have to want to fall, leave their minds, leave their illusions, and to face their own truth. They have to want to remember who they are again......

Boy: Why don't they do that?

Prospero: *(Long pause)*. Because they 'don't know' that they don't know their own truth. *(Seriously)*. They think that their illusion is true. They believe in the Answer.

Boy: *(Starts to speak but says nothing)*.

Prospero: I must go, now, Boy! *(Prospero turns abruptly, walks out the room leaving Boy sitting on his own)*.

Boy: *(Shocked).* They don't know they don't know! What to do! What to do......... *(Picks up his pencils, mutters to himself).*

Blackout

CPSIA information can be obtained
at www.ICGtesting.com
Printed in the USA
LVOW07s1535111217
559402LV00003B/909/P